# Choosing to Train

## Parenting Through Tough Times With Insight and Simplicity

Greg Smith, LCSW

Candace Couch, LPC

Edited by Sarah S. Johnson

Theological consultation with Matthew Currie, MDiv

Cover Design by Big Blue Creative

# PREFACE

Dear Reader,

In my many years of working with children and families, one thing has become abundantly clear: training children is simple and effective. Controlling children doesn't work and is crushing work for parents. Parents often insist on stressing themselves out by doing what God won't even do: controlling people. God allows us to choose our way. He faithfully informs us about our choices and the consequences and then allows us to choose. I think we should parent from His example: allowing children to make choices about their behavior and then standing by them as we provide the consequences.

I have spent my career working with the families of some of the most strong-willed children you will find. Early in my career, my mentor, Ronnie Weeks, taught me the value of avoiding power struggles with strong-willed children. I am indebted to him for teaching me this valuable truth—it is the foundation on which I have developed this model of parenting.

While the thoughts outlined in this book have proven to be helpful to families with strong-willed children, this method works for all children. This book is simply a model for lovingly and supportively helping children become good decision makers by training the prefrontal cortex in the work of analyzing the possible choices and the resulting consequences. All children need this type of training from their caregivers to prepare them for the road ahead.

Parenting from a training perspective rather than a controlling one requires intentionality and practice. It requires letting go of control of your child and, instead, choosing to train your child. It involves being different from many of your parenting peers. The five steps you will learn in this book will encourage you to slow down and make your parenting decisions simple and uncomplicated. Don't take on the anxieties that come along with attempting to control another human (it usually backfires anyway). I want you to remember to simply create opportunities to train your child by faithfully walking through the five simple steps outlined in this book. Take it easy and keep it simple.

Greg Smith, LCSW

# AUTHOR'S NOTE

The most common question asked of me at work is, "Where can I buy the book that will teach me more about this?" The answer (in my mind) has been, "In the hours and hours of meetings with my mentors," but I usually just reply that there isn't one. In the years between graduate school and private practice, I had the opportunity to work with my two professional mentors: Ronnie Weeks and Greg Smith. The offices we worked in became classrooms as my mentors taught me the art of counseling families. They taught me about power struggles, triangles, family structure, genograms, family rules and family roles. I learned about family conflict, scapegoats, defiant kids, anxiety, depression and emotional reactivity. Ronnie and Greg taught me most of what I know about counseling.

When Greg asked me to help him write this book, it provided two opportunities for me. First, I had the chance to finally provide a real answer to that question my clients have been asking me for years. This book has also rewarded me with the opportunity to give back to my mentor by documenting his very effective way of helping families change. I hope you find insight and encouragement in these pages. The parenting approach outlined in this book is applicable to the parents of defiant and compliant children and all the kids in between. Whether serious concerns about your child have brought you to this book, or you are simply hoping to increase the tools in your parental toolbox, I think you will find this information helpful and insightful. Parenting is not easy, but by finding the proper perspective and having a plan, the work becomes simplified and less complicated. This book is written to help parents do just that.
Keep up the good work!

Candace Couch, LPC

# CONTENTS

## Insight
Effective parents understand themselves.

1   Understanding Your Grid   1

2   Factors Impacting Your Grid   10

3   Positive Change For Your Grid   16

## Application
Parents who understand themselves can effectively train their children.

4   Factors Impacting Parenting   18

5   Choices and Consequences-The Five Simple Steps   28

6   Keep It Simple   35

7   Frequently Asked Questions   37

8   Quick Reference Guide   42

"Train up a child in the way he should go; even when he is old he will not depart from it."

Proverbs 22:6 (ESV)

## Choosing to Train

In my years of practice, two parenting skills have proven to be highly effective and have left clients and workshop attendees requesting a book that expounds upon the principles I teach. The first skill is identifying the parental desire to control kids, then intentionally choosing to train kids instead. This has a positive impact on the parent as an individual, the child as an individual and the relationship between the two. The second skill is teaching children about their ability to choose. It is essential that kids learn the value of decision-making skills since our lives are based on the continuous choices we make throughout the day. Choosing to train, however, reflects the need to not only help the child recognize and make choices, but to also make good choices as a parent. We are constantly faced with the decision to control or train the child and there begins the process of choices and consequences, with the choices and behavior of the parent.

# 1
# UNDERSTANDING YOUR GRID

"To know thyself is the beginning of wisdom." (Socrates)

or...

"To know thyself is the beginning of good parenting."

"Why do you look at the speck of sawdust in your brother's eye and pay no attention to the plank in your own eye? How can you say to your brother, 'Let me take the speck out of your eye,' when all the time there is a plank in your own eye? You hypocrite, first take the plank out of your own eye, and then you will see clearly to remove the speck from your brother's eye.
Matthew 7:3-5 (NIV)

## What Is Your Grid?

Why do you parent the way you do? Parenting and the conflicts that can accompany it can seem overwhelming and complicated. From the family that has silent, passive-aggressive power struggles to the family that is calling the police to help de-escalate a situation, none of it feels good or right. Families (parents and children) want peace, but their efforts to gain peace by getting their own way lead to conflict. Parents often come to counseling with hopes of sitting in the waiting room while the counselor works his/her magic in the counseling office so that the child reemerges a new, more mature version of the adolescent who entered. However, to understand the conflict that exists in a family you must understand the perspective of each individual family member. To understand the conflict between a parent and child, it is important to understand how the parent sees and interprets the world around him/her and what rules and expectations he/she has learned to survive in the world. As a result, parents spend just as much time in my counseling office as the child does. Sometimes, it's the child who gets to take a break in the waiting room while the parent does the challenging work of looking in the mirror and identifying the role he/she plays in relationships. To understand how to parent well, the parent must "know thyself."

Understanding yourself and how you parent based on your own developmental experience will also tell you a lot about how you relate to others in every other significant relationship you have, specifically marriage. The most influential element of how you operate as a parent is the "grid" through which you see the world. Your grid is your reality, the lens through which you see relationships, life choices, future plans, etc. The grid is the context for understanding the world around you. To understand why and how you parent (and to find ways to positively change your parenting style), you must look in the mirror and understand your grid.

The work of Alfred Adler, Albert Ellis and Aaron T. Beck helps us understand how the grid works. This is the basic premise of cognitive behavioral therapy. Life presents us with circumstances, which will be interpreted uniquely by the person experiencing the event. We interpret by thinking about the event, which leads to emotions. When we experience an emotion, we respond with a behavior. If the emotion is pleasant, we respond with a behavior that will maintain the emotion. If the emotion is unpleasant, we respond with a behavior that we think will make the emotion go away. For example, a person who is sitting on the dock at the lake at sunset and thinking about peacefulness and solitude will feel relaxed and content. The natural behavior would likely be to linger for as long as possible, rocking in the hammock, so that the positive emotion doesn't change. However, if a snake slithers onto the dock and the brain begins to think about the threats that a snake presents, fear develops and the behavior shifts to running away to safety. The goal of maintaining positive emotions and attempting to diminish negative emotions is developed from childhood. We have this same process while we parent. When my child is happy, quiet and content eating candy, I'm likely to indulge my child with more candy despite my conflicting thoughts about nutrition. My grid tells me two things: "quiet is good, do what it takes to keep it going," and, "nutrition is good, do what it takes to limit sugar intake for your child." The behavior I choose will be determined by the thoughts which creates the stronger emotion. Understanding your own grid (thought > emotion > behavior) will help you understand how and why you make the parenting choices you do and help you correct course where needed. Insight is the beginning of change.

The more informed we become about our own grid, the better able we are to understand our own choices as we interact with our children. As a result, we are then able to look past behaviors in our children (or anyone else we are in relationship with) and see the motivating factors. This creates an ability to be compassionate and empathetic while also being able to create opportunities for change in ourselves and family members.

## Survival With Position and Attention in The Family

To understand the grid we must understand that fear is the emotion that is most commonly avoided in our behavior. We learn during the developmental process what is required to survive (how to make sure that the family notices and gives the attention that is needed to survive.) Any perception that triggers fear makes us concerned that our survival is threatened. Behavior is then motivated by the desire to get rid of the fear.

In my experience working with families, current day "survival" is not a fight for food or dominance, but a fight for position (birth order or role) and attention. Position and attention is the necessary ingredient for survival. Parents have positive and negative attention to offer. Some children fight for positive attention and others fight for the negative. The child will also consistently work to maintain position in the family. We will talk more about birth order and family roles later. For example, the oldest child in a chaotic family may constantly work toward order or the youngest child in a family that is strict and rigid may always fight to be the "baby" by always looking for fun and a way to bend the family's rigid rules.

We must look at the grid with survival in mind. The child thinks "I must get my desired type of attention (positive or negative) or I go unnoticed (which creates fear)." Through training our children we expose them to the stimuli that trigger fear (not getting the attention they desire or maintaining their typical position in the family) and prove to them that they can survive it. They can face fear and live. The most valuable lesson is that they will be just fine and actually become healthier when they are gaining appropriate attention in appropriate ways. This also requires that parents are mindful of providing appropriate attention and training behaviors that trigger negative attention. The oldest child from the earlier example will find that he can survive when things are disorderly. He can trust his parents to manage the chaos--it's not all up to him. The youngest child in the rigid family will learn that she can survive life with rules and that parents can balance structure and fun. She doesn't have to create her own fun through rebellion. We will talk more about the process of training later in the book.

### Case Study in Attention, Position, Fear and Survival

Meet Defiant Dylan. After his parents' divorce, he felt tremendous fear. How would he survive this change in his family? Would they still love and take care of him? His perception of the divorce as a threat to his survival creates fear. The fear is uncomfortable and to reduce this feeling he decides that he will become difficult and defiant, proving to his parents that this divorce was a terrible idea. If he chooses to be compliant and recover well from the divorce, he fears he could be condoning his parents' decision. He determines to send the message that he disagrees with their decision loud and clear, through his defiant behavior. As we will discuss later, if Dylan's defiant behavior is rewarded with loads of negative attention (meetings with teachers, endless lectures about his behavior, etc.), his behavior is perpetuated. If Dylan's parents learn to not give excessive negative attention for his behavior, but choose to train this behavior with choices and consequences, Dylan learns that defiant behavior doesn't benefit him through attention. It only results in consequences. Then his parents are allowed the opportunity to provide appropriate, positive attention at times that are unrelated to Dylan's defiance.

## Thoughts on Middle Children and Attention

Often when middle children present for counseling it is because the child is very reactive and angry. In most cases, the reactive middle child learns that the only way to get attention is to make noise. Just as the saying goes, "the squeaky wheel gets the oil." To make noise, the child decides to be defiant, angry or tantrums often. This behavior does not always have to look like defiance. When the middle child is fighting for attention, they will demonstrate many types of behavior that are out of the norm and often cause parents concern. The older child may be getting attention for doing well and the baby is getting attention for being cute (like the babies always are). The middle child's grid informs him that if he is quiet and compliant he won't get the attention that feels necessary for survival. Therefore, he engages in behavior that will gain attention.

## How is the Grid Developed?

Grid development starts at birth based on your interaction with your family of origin, which includes parents, siblings and other significant caregivers. The grid is as unique and intricate as a fingerprint. Children who come from the same family of origin will develop different (sometimes extremely different) or similar grids based on birth order, relationship with parents/caregivers, family roles and trauma or addiction in a significant member of the family.

Your experience of reality is based on perceptions about life that were developed in early childhood. This is when you start to see and understand the world around you and can learn from the feedback loops you experience. These are the rules you are learning to help you survive in your world.

Let's examine the possible development of Patty Perfectionist's grid. At age four, Patty's demanding and rigid parent lashes out in rage after she spills her milk. She becomes fearful of her parent's anger and makes the learning connection between accidents and other people's anger. Her emotional response is fear (guilt, regret and feelings of being a disappointment), which leads her to behave in an over-responsible way—making sure she never spills milk again to avoid that feeling of fear (guilt/regret/disappointment) when her parent becomes angry. Her grid now informs her that accidents are to be feared, so she must live perfectly so that no accidents occur in the future. And so begins her battle with balancing fear, perfectionism, over-responsibility and anxiety.

## Why Does the Grid Matter?

Once we have an understanding of our own grid and the grid of our child, we are then able to create change. We are able to put ourselves and others into situations that disprove the "survival skill." These circumstances show us that the survival skills are no longer necessary or effective. For example, when Defiant Dylan's parents no longer reward his defiant behavior with unlimited attention by lecturing and instead choose to train him by simply providing consequences for his behavior and appropriate attention at times unrelated to his negative behavior, the likelihood of Dylan's behavior changing increases. The goal becomes to take away the reward for the behavior. In parenting, the reward for behaviors can be giving-in or becoming reactive (anger, shutting down or withdrawing). Even our facial expressions can serve as a reward for the child's behavior. Change occurs when misery from the consequence of the behavior is greater than the fear or discomfort that may come with change. The idea of change may be appealing but trying something new goes against our grid. Our thoughts (and family and friends) will draw us back to our original grid. The process of change will require confronting fears, dealing with the discomfort of trying new things and "upsetting the apple cart" when others would prefer that we behave in our old ways.

## Case Study of Family Grids

Johnny has become an excessive whiner. It sounds like he has forgotten how to talk and make requests in his normal 8-year-old, adorable little voice. He has become convinced that the better option is to use a high-pitched whining noise to voice his complaints and requests. Johnny's mom and dad are annoyed by this behavior and are determined that it must change.

Before they start the process of training that behavior, it becomes necessary to understand the parents' grids and how they interact with Johnny's grid to reward and perpetuate the behavior.

Let's take an honest look at mom's grid. Mom is the youngest child in her family-of-origin who was loved and adored and was easily compliant because she was consistently indulged. She rarely faced situations where people would not do what she wanted and when she did she became frustrated and withdrew from the relationship after making her annoyance clear. These days when Johnny begins to whine, Mom gets annoyed and shows her annoyance with the grimace on her face. She then huffs and puffs and sighs. She knows that there are two ways this situation will go: she will soon just withdraw to escape the annoyance by retreating to her room (and slamming the door!) or Dad will jump in and fix the problem for her. Either way the problem will soon not be hers to deal with anymore. Just a few more slams and stomps and she won't have to listen to Johnny's whining.

Let's look at Dad's grid. Dad is an oldest child who was compliant because he loves the praise and adoration that achievement and compliance earned him from his parents, teachers, coaches and everyone he came in contact with. He learned that he could always earn admiration by fixing other people's problems. When Johnny whines, Dad knows it causes a problem for Mom and he springs into action to fix the problem. He will begin to reason and bargain with Johnny to smooth things over and stop the whining. Sometimes that may mean taking Johnny outside to play to get Johnny out of Mom's hair. Dad's alternative goal is to not let mom get to that place where she makes her annoyance obvious to everyone and then withdraws. Dad knows that he must accommodate Johnny and stop the whining before it makes a mess of their day with Mom. As a result, Johnny's whining behavior is reinforced by Dad taking him outside to play.

Let's look at Johnny's grid. Johnny becomes fearful when he doesn't get his way. He has learned that he can whine and make Mom mad which will end in two possibilities: she will withdraw, at which point he is off the hook and never really held accountable for his behavior, or Dad will jump in to save the day and indulge him to his heart's delight in an effort to get him to stop whining and keep Mom happy and engaged with the family. Johnny knows how to get his reward (Mom mad and withdrawing and Dad focused completely on Johnny and all of his wishes).

To help Mom and Dad train Johnny's behavior, we have to see the reward that Johnny is pursuing and then make that reward no longer an option. When mom stops withdrawing and is willing to step in and effectively train Johnny's behavior, the reward for the whining stops and the consequences Mom provides decreases Johnny's desire to whine. Also, when Dad stops stepping in to save the day for Mom by indulging Johnny, the controlling stops and the training begins. Instead, Dad can provide Johnny with the choices about whining and inform him of the consequences that will result from his choices. We will talk about this more in the Choice and Consequence section. The focus here is to see that to train Johnny's behavior we must look at the grid of everyone involved in the family.

Through understanding our grids we are able to become aware of how and why we reward concerning or bad behavior in our children. Then we are able to change our grid. Mom and Dad can respond differently and prove that they will in fact survive if they try new behavior other than their survival behavior (Mom's withdrawal and Dad's indulgence). Also Mom and Dad are able to create experiences for Johnny to find out he can survive in this family without whining. Mom can stay engaged without becoming angry and Johnny can receive positive attention from Dad without having to whine.

# 2
# FACTORS IMPACTING YOUR GRID

## Birth Order

Birth order can be a hotly debated theory. However, in the family counseling context it often proves essential for understanding one's grid. There are exceptions which can often be traced to situations of trauma, illness, abuse, neglect, abandonment or addiction in the family of origin. In Dr. Kevin Leman's book, *The Birth Order Book*, he provides an astonishingly accurate description of birth order and its impact on relationships and a person's understanding of the world:

> "[First Born:] perfectionistic, reliable, conscientious, list maker, well organized, hard driving, natural leader, critical, serious, scholarly, logical, doesn't like surprises...
>
> [Middle Child:] mediator, compromising, diplomatic, avoids conflict, independent, loyal to peers, many friends, a maverick, secretive, unspoiled
>
> [Last Born/Baby:] manipulative, charming, blames others, attention seeker, tenacious, people person, natural salesperson, precocious, engaging, affectionate, loves surprises
>
> [Only Child:] little adult by age seven, very thorough, deliberate, high achiever, self-motivated, fearful, cautious, voracious reader, black and white thinker...can't bear to fail, has high expectations of self,

more comfortable with people who are older or younger"[1]

Of course, there are times when these characteristics don't play out in a family and then we must look closer to see what was so important in the family that members had to develop differently. This is when is it helpful to look at family roles.

**Family Roles**

If the standard birth order descriptions don't play out in a family, it may be because of trauma such as illness, death, loss, abuse, neglect, addiction, financial issues, divorce, etc.

To help make sense of family dynamics in families where birth order does not play out, it is helpful to look at the roles that family members play. Family roles are typical and can be healthy[2]. A healthy family will have members who operate in certain roles and may change from one role to another based on the needs or demands of the family[2]. When trauma or addiction are present, these roles can become more solidified and are not as fluid and flexible but rigid and necessary to the survival of the family. In the book, *Love is A Choice,* by Hemfelt, Minirth and Meier, the roles are described as layers within the family: "The foundation layers are the universal relationships such a mother/daughter or sister/sister. The roles of hero, and so on, form a second layer upon the first and are healthy unless carried to extreme as a coping mechanism."[2]

Here are some examples of commonly occurring family roles:

Hero
Heroes are here to save the day! They will do whatever it takes to fix the problem that may exist in the family and they usually gain attention (and sometimes distract from the issues that need to be addressed) by achievement in academics, sports, relationships, church, or any other possible areas of success. If there is an opportunity for achievement they will sniff it out and if there is an opportunity to fix the family they will sacrifice their own health and peace to try to make it happen. Children who are heroes are often seen as mature and responsible, and parents will give them power

and responsibility that is too great for their developmental level. While the child may gladly take on this power and responsibility at the time, it often has a negative impact in the long run. Heroes develop a grid that informs them they are in charge and can control relationships and situations. When things don't go well they perceive it as their fault and will deal with guilt that is not theirs to carry.

## Scapegoat

First, let's look at Merriam-Webster's definition of scapegoat: "one that bears the blame of others; one that is the object of irrational hostility."[3]

This is true for the family scapegoat. The scapegoat is reacting to the circumstances of the family with behavior that everyone will point to as wrong or bad. However, the family often perpetuates the scapegoat's behavior by providing negative attention. Scapegoats learn to get their need for attention met through negative attention. Scotty Scapegoat asks his mother, "why do my brothers have to go to school?" when he is at home during the day and missing his older brothers who are at school. Instead of answering the question calmly, the mother furrows her brow and scolds the child saying, "All of my children WILL get an education!" As Scotty gets older and seeks negative attention, he will forever bring up how stupid school is when he needs attention from his mom. He knows that topic will get a reaction from her. He knows that to gain attention from his mom he must skip school, fail classes and talk about how he can't wait to drop out. When Scotty feels negative emotions, he will move toward this scapegoat behavior because misery loves company and he knows he can make his mom miserable. The behavior of a scapegoat may be what caused you to read this book.

## Baby

The baby is cute and lovable and receives attention just by being adorable. The baby is often indulged because of the parent's lack of ability to provide attention because of older siblings or the parents' fatigue related to parenting. Either way the baby is often spoiled and demanding. This does not mean that the baby will always act bratty. This spoiled and demanding grid may be internal and on the outside the baby acts compliant and happy while internally becoming frustrated that those outside the family of origin do not give them the attention they "deserve."

When the oldest chooses to not be the hero in the family (possibly due to trauma, divorce, addiction or health issues) the baby can take on the hero role. The baby becomes "the baby hero" who learns that attention can be gained by not only being lovable and cute but also through achievement, caregiving and peacekeeping in relationships.

### Lost Child

The lost child senses tension easily and chooses to escape. While the hero may try to fix and the baby may try to distract, the lost child disappears to avoid dealing with the issues that are present in the family. This disappearing may happen into video games, books, sleep or relationships outside of the family.

### Peacekeeper

The peacekeeper spends a great deal of energy on making sure the family environment remains peaceful. The peacekeeper will avoid the truth, look the other way, fix and ask others to do the same (directly or indirectly) in an effort to avoid the conflict or tension that exists in the family. The peacekeeper has an unconscious (and sometimes conscious) belief that the family can't handle the realities of their situation and if the conflict erupted the family would be unable to recover. Therefore, peace must be maintained despite the toll it takes on the members of the family.

### Rebel

The rebel calls "bull" on the injustices and unspoken rules in the family. The family makes their best efforts of making the rebel get in line with their rules and ways of doing things. The rebel's rebellion doesn't have to be drugs and wild parties. Sometimes the rebellion can simply be refusal to go to church for the fifth time this week.

### Family Roles in Relation to Addiction

In the case of a family dealing with addiction, the family members would like for the addict to get clean or sober. They have learned to function in a way to maintain peace and some sense of order within the family despite the addict's unpredictable behavior. Family members often describe it as "walking on eggshells" or "keeping the peace." The goal is to prevent chaos but the side-effect is that the family prevents the addict from experiencing the true consequences of his/her unhealthy behavior. The family is absorbing these consequences at the cost of their own emotional health. These family members are often seen in counseling with severe anxiety or depression because of the long-term effects of trying to maintain order in a family where chaos could erupt at any time. Family members in this role are often dealing with enabling or codependent tendencies.

There are emotional payoffs for the enabler as well. They feel needed and useful. There is meaning in their life: helping the person struggling with addiction, keeping the family stable, making sure everything is ok. They can often feel capable and in control and to take that away is a change in identity that is difficult to deal with. When the alcoholic husband/father begins recovery and stays sober, changes take place in the daily life and overall identity of the others in the family.

These family roles don't just show up in families that deal with addiction. Milder dynamics in families can create very similar dynamics: an angry parent, a workaholic parent, image/reputation driven parents, anxious parents. The list goes on and on. These roles develop in families who experience stress on any level of the spectrum. The more stressed the family becomes, the more deeply entrenched the roles will become. In families who are dealing with milder stress, the roles are flexible and can change based on circumstances. As stress in the family intensifies, the family members adapt by further developing their given role[2].

Some may call these roles or these families dysfunctional. I choose not to because the roles serve a very specific function: preventing the destruction of the family. For example, the wife of an alcoholic husband may call in sick for her husband who is not sick, but unable to go to work because of his drinking. Her behavior enables his destructive behavior by making it possible for him to miss work without having to make the call to his boss to explain the reason himself. The wife's behavior is functional for the family because it prevents or delays possible financial or social consequences for the family (ie. loss of job or embarrassment because of his irresponsibility). While the wife's role as the enabler (or hero) may be functional, it is not healthy. It requires that she take responsibility for things that are not her responsibility. This often causes resentment in relationships. It also prevents the husband from experiencing the consequences of his behavior (job loss, financial consequences, social consequences, etc.). When the natural consequences of a choice are prevented, the person making the choice is shielded from the impact of the consequences and will not choose differently in the future. The training experiences of choices and their consequences are prevented and the crisis moments that call people to change is delayed.

# 3
# POSITIVE CHANGE FOR YOUR GRID

## How Can the Grid Be Changed?

Changing your grid requires taking an honest look at your behaviors and the emotions and perceptions that fuel them. Then, you must look at the consequences of your chosen behaviors. If you want the consequences to change you must change your perceptions and behaviors. In the earlier case study with Johnny, Mom realized that her withdrawal or expressions of anger perpetuated Johnny's whining. As she understands her grid and seeks to change it, she realizes she can stay engaged but she also must address her thinking to change the way that she perceives the situation. As she grows in insight about her grid, she realizes that her withdrawal behavior is a survival skill from her family of origin that always led to her getting what she wanted. She now recognizes that as an adult her choice to withdraw or act out her anger does not get her what she wants. It only leads to disconnection from her son and putting her husband in a position to over-indulge their son. This withdrawal and angry behavior served her well in childhood but is no longer appropriate. When she is tempted to perceive Johnny's behavior as frustrating, she chooses to think about her opportunity to train him with her appropriate behavior by staying engaged and calm and providing him with choices and consequences. She is an adult now and no longer needs to use her old survival skills to get her way. When she perceives her world in this new way she feels calm and behaves in a more appropriate and healthy manner toward Johnny and her husband. In order to change her grid, Mom worked hard to change her perceptions (thinking), and as a result, her emotions and behaviors change.

# 4
# FACTORS IMPACTING PARENTING

## The Elements of Parenting With Choice and Consequence

When we are aware of our grid and how it impacts our behavior, we are able to make informed choices about all behavior, including parenting. To make wise and effective parenting decisions, we must do the work of understanding our perceptions, the emotions they create and the resulting behavior. In the process of parenting, when we feel negative emotions, our behavior toward our children becomes controlling and not training. Controlling our kids has negative emotional impacts on the relationship in the short-term and long-term. For strong-willed or defiant kids, controlling behavior from the parent is a cue for the child to dig his/her heels in and become increasingly stubborn and/or defiant. Then the power struggle begins.

Before learning the five steps of training, we must become more aware of what controlling parenting behavior looks like so we know to stop it when it rears its head. First we will look at typical parenting styles that are based on controlling children and then compare training and control.

## Parenting Styles

The parenting styles that follow are humorous and accurate descriptions of the roles that parents take on when attempting to control their child's behavior. Read through and see if you can relate to any of these styles.

The Nun
Control over the child is attempted through shaming the child for undesirable behavior.

The result is.. the child feels shame. ("That's terrible that you would even think about doing that to your sister!")

The Preacher
This parent attempts to control by sharing overwhelming amounts of information through lectures and sermons. These sermons and lectures can be mild or loud. Either way, they are attempts to control rather than train.

The result is...the child feels stupid ("you should have known better") or guilty ("you are supposed to set a good example").

The Chihuahua
This parent has a lot of "bark" with very little power or follow-through. The barking can include constant reminders or nagging about desired behaviors, but without consistent consequences that provide training.

The result is...the child learns that the parent doesn't mean what they say. In other words, the parent lies to their child with empty threats.

The Henchman
This parent has to finish the work that was started by someone else. One parent makes the threat and then the henchman has to do the dirty work. An example would be the mom who says, "wait 'til your father gets home."

The result is...the child feels resentment because the mother started the fight and calls in the father to finish it. The child isn't able to work conflict all the way to resolve with one person. Being able to work through conflict together is a valuable lesson for children to learn with their parents.

The Bully
The bullying parent uses intimidation instead of training. An example would be the parent who says, "you aren't going to disrespect me in my house!"

The result is...the child's respect decreases for the parent.

The Interrogator
This parent works as a private investigator in attempts to control behavior by minimizing surprises and always trying to be "in the know" about the child's behavior. This parent also wants a confession and acknowledgement of what their child did wrong. An example would be, "So...did anything happen at school today?" (school already called to tell the parent what happened).

The result is...the child learns quickly that the best option to survive life with this parent is to lie.

If any of these seem familiar, don't fret. Knowing your tendency to control and how you play that out with your child is the first step in letting go of control and turning your attention and effort toward training your child.

**Parental Desire for Control**

To grasp the process of training, it is important to understand the nuances of both training and control. Let's look at a brief comparison of the two concepts on the chart on the next page.

| Training is.. | Control is... |
|---|---|
| slow | fast |
| process-oriented | content/results oriented |
| a lifetime focus | a now focus |
| grace-giving | shaming |
| heart/mind-focused | behavior-focused |
| seeing the value of and allowing the crash/failure/misbehavior | devaluing and preventing the crash/failure/misbehavior |
| growing humility in the parent | feeding fear and pride in the parent |
| decreasing rebellion/unhealthy compliance in the child | increasing rebellion/unhealthy compliance in the child |
| painful for the parent | painful for the child |
| letting go of the child, results, grades, good behavior, your reputation/expectations | holding onto the child, results, grades, good behavior, your reputation/expectations |
| predictable<br>Wise choices (independent of parental influences) are eventually the result of consistent, disciplined training. | unpredictable<br>May or may not result in good behavior this time...who knows what will happen next time. |
| the child chooses his/her behavior which teaches lifelong decision-making skills | the parent chooses the child's behavior so the child doesn't develop decision making skills |

When parents choose to train, they choose to continue to be faithful to training no matter what the outcome. Even if the child consistently makes choices that the parent wishes were different, the parent doesn't give up. Consistency is key. Training parents realize that it's not about the training "working" (ie, the child makes the choices parents want them to make). It's about being faithful to training and creating predictable and consistent consequences so that the child has time to practice decision making in a safe setting. Training parents also realize they can't control their child's behavior. All they can control is whether they train or control. It's not about good and bad behavior. It's about whether or not the child experienced a consistent consequence and is using consequences as data for future decision-making.

### Saying "Yes!"-The Permissive Spirit of Letting Go of Control

Training parents use "yes" language instead of constantly telling their kids "no, no, no". They acknowledge their child's ability to make his/her own choices and simply help him/her remember what the consequences will be for those choices (whether natural or established by the parents). For example, "Yes, you can choose to do that but…you will also be choosing [consequence.] Using "yes" language doesn't mean that you are encouraging your child to do these things. It simply acknowledges what your child's choices are and helps them see the consequences of those choices. 1 Corinthians 10:23 says, "'I have the right to do anything,' you say —but not everything is beneficial. 'I have the right to do anything' —but not everything is constructive." (NIV) Throughout the Bible God shows that we have choices about how we live. He faithfully helps us understand the consequences of those choices as well. Jesus reinforced this concept in Matthew 7:13: "Enter through the narrow gate. For wide is the gate and broad is the road that leads to destruction, and many enter through it. But small is the gate and narrow the road that leads to life, and only a few find it." (NIV) Jesus is informing us of the choices that exist and the decision about the gate and road we choose is ours.

The easiest test to determine if you are a controlling parent is to ask the question, do you want your child to mess up, or do you want them to do what you want them to do? A training parent desires their children to mess up because they understand that consequences train behavior. The failures that take place in the safety of the family train the child in wise decision making in life outside the family.

Have you ever boarded a plane and after looking at your pilot's welcoming face, wondered what his days of training were like? Is he the compliant oldest-child hero in his family who wanted to do everything right? Did his grid play out in flight school where he studied hard, followed all the directions with accuracy and never made a mistake? Did he never have to face the crash landing in the flight simulator because he did everything right and the crash was never necessary? I want my pilot to have experienced the crash simulation so that if worst comes to worst, he knows how to make choices in that scenario. His compliance and achievement will be meaningless if he doesn't know how to make the difficult choices when it comes to flying my plane. This is an exaggerated example, of course, but this is true with our children. If we control them into compliance they never face the opportunities of dealing with a "crash." They never gain the learning that comes with making the connection between their choice and the consequences they must endure. If we prevent the crash, we hijack the training. When training, the trainer wants the crash. That is where the learning begins.

As controlling parents, we want to prevent the crash. We want our kids to be compliant achievers who do all the things right. Then, we never have to watch them endure the consequences that result from their poor choices. When they achieve and comply, we feel good about ourselves and look good to others. We want to use consequences to indulge our own anger toward them instead of using consequences in a way that is separate from our emotional expression. When consequences are used to control, we use them to express our anger toward children instead of dealing with emotions independently of consequences. We will talk about what to do with emotions later in the book.

## Why Do We Control?

We control because of our grid as discussed earlier in this book. Often, we control when our perceptions of the situation lead us to fear because there is a threat to our pride (embarrassment). Our family roles and birth order will also determine when we choose to control. For example, heroes will control when their accomplishments and success depend on the behavior of another person. If their child threatens their hero status by making decisions that will reflect poorly upon the hero parent, the parent must face the fear and humiliation. To escape the fear and maintain their pride they must control their child into compliance.

When you are ready to let go of control and the frustrations and anxieties that result, then you are ready to provide training for your child. Using choices and consequences is not using consequences to control your child.

## Emotions (Yours and Theirs) and Training

As we discuss the elements of training behavior, keep in mind that it is necessary to attend to emotion while providing this training. To provide choices and consequences without attending to a child's emotions is to simply provide punishment. The goal is to provide emotional intelligence skills so the child begins to see his/her own grid while also helping him/her understand the concept of choices and their consequences.

When we train, instead of control, we have the relational resources to use empathy and validate the child's emotions because we aren't busy being defensive and arguing our own point. When we control, instead of train, we communicate the following message: "I don't care about what you think or how you feel. Just act right."

When there is a concerning behavior, it is helpful to ask which parent has done this behavior in the past or had a family member who had a similar behavior. We ask this because children will do what they are trained to do. We train our kids into behaviors that we desire and, paradoxically, we train them into those that we do not want. We train them through the rewards that we intentionally and unintentionally give. For example, the emotional reactions of a parent (even negative ones, like anger) can train a child into continuing in the behavior that brings about the emotional reaction. As a result, when using the choice-consequence technique, we become aware of parental emotional reaction and try to eliminate it in an effort to remove rewards that perpetuate undesirable behavior in the child. Parents begin to manage their own emotions and not bring them into the interaction with the child. This decreases the complication of managing the parent's emotions, child's emotions and the situation. That is too much to address all at once! Instead, our goal is to deal with parental emotions separately from dealing with the child's behavior. Parents should identify their emotional reaction to their child's behavior and explore how this plays into their grid. When the parent has gained insight about his/her emotions and is not looking to explode with his/her emotions toward the child, he/she is able to attend to the situation in a calm way. When we understand our grid and can choose not to be emotionally reactive with kids, we dodge the power struggle and have opportunities to attend to the emotions of our kids instead of only focusing on behaviors. Here is an example of what this might sound like: Sassy Sandy pushes her sister as she walks out of the kitchen. Her insightful mom takes time to think about how watching that behavior impacts her own grid. Mom is the oldest child and is triggered by Sandy's carelessness and disregard for the rules. Mom realizes that she feels angry because of her perception of Sandy's behavior. She chooses to address her perception and reframe this as an opportunity to train Sandy about the consequences of pushing others. She realizes that acting out her anger would actually cause disconnection from Sandy and hijack the training process. Mom calmly says to Sandy, "You know that in our family we choose to lose our phone for 24 hours if we push someone. I realize that you were frustrated with your sister and that you will be sad and disappointed to lose your phone. I would be too. I'm sorry. Please put your phone on the kitchen counter. You can pick it back up at this time tomorrow."

When a child or adolescent detects (and their detectors are sensitive and accurate) that he/she is being controlled, often, his/her goal becomes to make the parent angry in order to stop the control. A child angers the parent by misbehaving (being defiant, disrespectful or anything else they know creates anger in the parent's grid). The parent then acts out his/her anger (stink eye, yelling, silent treatment, etc.) and the behavior has been rewarded. The goal was achieved. The child made the controlling parent experience and act out their negative emotions. The parent erroneously thinks that his/her angry behavior toward the child will teach the child to not misbehave again. The parent is wrong. Mom or Dad has encouraged the behavior for the future. The child has made the learning connection that misbehaving stops the parent's controlling behavior by making the parent angry and relationally distancing the parent from the child. There are two places of intervention to stop the child's undesirable behavior: decrease parental control (causing the child to not feel controlled which leads to misbehavior) and changing the parent's emotional reactivity to the misbehavior; therefore, decreasing the reward.

When using the choice-consequence technique, it is important to keep your grid in mind at all times. Realizing that when you are triggered by your child's behavior and start to experience strong negative emotions, you will default to your old survival techniques and neglect your new, healthy parenting techniques. When triggered, you will reach for control and, as a result, miss an opportunity to train your child. Keeping your grid and your child's grid in mind while using choices and consequences will also help prevent you from providing rewards that will prevent training. For example, in our case study of family grids, Johnny's reward for whining was that Mom withdrew, leaving all of Dad's attention (and indulgence) on Johnny. As Mom and Dad use the choices and consequences model, they will want to prevent the rewards that they created in their old process. Mom will choose to stay engaged and manage her anger. She will reframe Johnny's whining from being a reminder of how she isn't getting the peace and quiet she deserves to simply a behavior that requires training. Just as baby Johnny required training with drinking from a cup and eating with a spoon, older Johnny requires training to stop whining. Mom will be able to stay engaged and not leave Dad on his own to control Johnny into compliance. Dad will need to keep in mind that while his old grid told him to make everyone happy even if that meant becoming permissive with Johnny, his new grid requires that he face his fear of others' disapproval and disappointment. Johnny won't be happy that he isn't rewarded in the way that he expects. Mom may become disappointed that Dad is no longer stopping the whining by controlling Johnny. Dad will face his fear and effectively train the behavior instead of controlling Johnny's behavior. Training will be slow and require many episodes of practice, but it provides an opportunity for Johnny, Mom and Dad to grow, mature and become a healthier family.

The overall goal is to keep this process simple. The parent is not controlling the child's behavior, but creating training opportunities by helping the child clearly understand what the choices are and what the consequences of each choice will be. We don't control with reminders and threats about the consequences. Following God's example with us, we allow them to choose. Then we stay with them emotionally as we provide the consequences, or as they experience the natural consequences that result. Training parents don't make their own emotional reactivity (anger, frustration, etc.) the consequence. Training parents maintain an emotional connection while consistently providing consequences.

# 5
# CHOICES AND CONSEQUENCES-
# THE FIVE SIMPLE STEPS

1. Identify your conviction and keep it to yourself.

Convictions are the traits that you would desire your child to possess when he/she leaves your home and enters the world (ie. strong work ethic, manners, good hygiene, spiritual practices, etc.) Most parents try to talk their children into having these characteristics through lecturing and nagging instead of training their child in behaviors that may lead the child to develop these convictions on their own.

**Biblical Wisdom About Forcing Parental Convictions on Kids**
It is most effective when parents work together to identify convictions and the behaviors they want to train. This helps determine which battles they will choose. When parents disagree on what behaviors they are training, the training becomes ineffective because of the inconsistency. Parents will address the behavior with consequences sometimes but not all the time and create confusion about whether or not that consequence is the result of their chosen behavior. Any inconsistency or disagreement between parents about what behaviors need to be trained also creates opportunities for children to play the parents against each other.

Parents must spend time identifying exactly what core values and life skills they believe are important for their child to know before leaving home.

Many parents want to lecture and educate their children about the convictions they have about behavior. Unfortunately, children and teenagers tend to tune these lectures out and the energy expended in these efforts is wasted. In Matthew 7:6 Jesus says, "Do not give dogs what is sacred; do not give pearls to pigs. If you do, they may trample them under their feet and turn and tear you to pieces (NIV)." To apply this Biblical wisdom to parenting a "pearl" in this case is any wisdom handed to a kid that they don't think they need. For instance, a mother tries to encourage a child to work on their project that is due three weeks from now. The child, who does not agree with pre-planning and working ahead of schedule, will stomp that pearl of wisdom (planning ahead and accomplishing tasks with an organized timeline) in the mud and "tear the mom to pieces" with conflict and relational distance. Instead of nagging and reminding (which are subtle attempts to control) the mom could set up choices and consequences that reflect her convictions about pre-planning and work ethic. She may say, "Yes, you can choose when you work on your project, but each day that you choose not to work on it is a day you choose to go without your video game time. I'm ok with you not working on it if you are ok with not playing video games."

It is great to share your wisdom with your child when they want to learn the lesson. Offering them wisdom when they don't want it creates relational conflict. Training is a better option during these times. Parents don't have to waste time and energy in the frustrating task of forcing wisdom on a person who does not want it. Also, kids are spared the relational distancing that is created when they endure a lecture. Training creates opportunities for kids to ask questions and pursue the wisdom themselves instead of having it forced on them. Share wisdom during times when there is no conflict and you and your child are enjoying the conversation.

Sharing your wisdom in small doses is helpful too. Many times parents pursue their child to give them their wisdom. Try switching the roles of pursuer and pursued by saying "I actually know a lot about ____(insert topic you wish to discuss)____. Let me know if you ever want to hear about it." Example: "I actually know a lot about drugs. Let me know if you want to talk about it." Here is another example of changing the parent's need to give information into the child's need to have the information: The father who demands that his son get out in the hot August afternoon heat for a lesson in changing the tire becomes a heated battle of wills between the controlling father ("my son WILL learn how to change a tire today") and the reluctant son. This father could change the pursuer/pursued dynamic by letting the air out of his son's tire and waiting on his son to ask about what should happen next. This is an extreme example, but an encouragement to look for ways to create a desire in the child to obtain wisdom instead of trying to force wisdom into the resistant child.

Parents can also become very concerned about their child's attitude and heart. A person's attitude is the outward expression of the heart. The child's attitude gives us visual and auditory data about what is going on in their heart. We cannot train their heart. The heart is part of the soul that is off limits to other human beings. Jesus has full access to the soul and the child's heart, so we will learn to trust him with this area of the child. All we can train is the behavior. This is the area of parenting that we are given the responsibility to be consistent and faithful to: the training of the child's behavior. We can show care, concern and love for their heart and soul but we can trust God with creating change in these areas of the child's life.

The difference between training and control is that the consequences do the teaching, not your lectures, explanations and reasoning.

2. Identify behavior: What behavior are you training?

Be clear with yourself about what you are focusing on. This is the behavior that has triggered a reaction or concern in you because it is inconsistent with your convictions. Examples may include disrespectful talk, inappropriate use of technology, homework refusal, not doing chores, etc. Becoming very specific about the behavior you are training helps you avoid spending time on other behaviors that are not currently being addressed. For example, if your child forgets to do a chore this week but he typically does it each week this would not be an area that you would focus on training. You would spend your energy focusing on behavior that is regularly causing an issue for your child, yourself and the family.

3. Give Grace the First Time and Set It Up For the Future

Give grace the first time the child does the targeted behavior, because consequences that are not perceived as the child's choice create resentment. Once you have identified a behavior you are training, the next time the child does the behavior you can give the warning. Even if your child has done this same behavior hundreds of times before, this is the first time you will show grace and educate him/her about his/her future choices with this behavior. Invite him/her to continue the negative behavior and inform him/her of the consequence: "You can (insert behavior) but next time you will be choosing ___ consequence ___." For example, "You can choose to speak disrespectfully to me and the next time you do you will choose to spend 20 minutes doing chores with me." This is a great time to offer alternatives as well. For example: "Or you can choose to speak respectfully and you will be choosing to continue on with your day without 20 minutes of extra chores."

4. Allow the Choice

This is their opportunity to choose! Warning: you will feel a desire to control through reminders, lectures, emotional reactions (becoming angry, acting sad/disappointed/withdrawing, etc.)
Sit back and keep it simple. Let your child choose.

This is also the stage where you must do your own emotional work. You will deal with the disappointment, sadness, frustration, etc. that is associated with watching your child make the choice you didn't want them to make and then deal with the process of providing the consequences. This "emotional work" requires that you practice emotional intelligence by identifying how you feel, what caused you to feel that way and the choices you have in front of you about how to behave while you feel this way. You, the parent, have your own choices and consequences to consider.

For example, I can choose to blow up at my child telling them all the reasons why what they have done was wrong and lecture them about how this is all their fault. Or I can choose to approach the situation without emotional reactivity. My child has a choice about his/her behavior and I, as a parent, have a choice about my behavior.

5. Provide the Consequence

Example: "You chose to speak disrespectfully to me, so you chose to spend 20 minutes helping me with chores today. I'll set the timer. Let's get started."

Remember the effective consequence is not your emotional reaction. Their choice is not a personal attack and does not have personal meaning about you as a parent. Their choice means that they are still learning and being trained in decision making. Stay calm and give the consequence. Don't give lectures or emotional reactions. This will only confuse the child and prevent effective training. Stay connected to the child emotionally and relationally. When we choose sin, God does not leave us or punish us with his angry outbursts. He loves us and stays near and continues to train us through the consequences that our sinful choices bring.

Keep in mind that children will put emotions between choices and consequences. They can get so hurt or angry that nothing (no matter the severity of the consequence) will deter their negative behavior. For example, after Defiant Diana's parents' divorce, she changed from a reasonable and compliant child to consistently defiant. She was hurt and confused by her parents' divorce but didn't have the emotional vocabulary to express that to them. Instead, she punishes her parents for their decision with her defiant behavior. As long as the hurt and confusion are driving her behavior, her behavior doesn't change, no matter what the consequences are. Her parents' job isn't to find the most severe consequence that will convince her not to be defiant (that would be controlling). Since her parents are committed to train her, they will consistently provide consequences for her defiant behavior while managing their own emotional reaction to the behavior and attending to Diana's emotions as well. This may sound like, "Diana, you chose to speak disrespectfully again. You know that means you've chosen to help me with chores for 20 minutes. I've noticed that you've been speaking disrespectfully a lot more since the divorce. I'm wondering if you are angry or hurt with me." It is ok if consequences do not appear to be changing behavior. Remain faithful to the process of helping a child clearly understand his/her choices and the consequences. Success is not defined by the child's compliant behavior. Success is defined as the parent's faithfulness to the process of providing choices and consequences.

Here are some things to consider as you choose to train instead of control your child:

## Emotions

Don't include a subtle emotional consequence along with the actual consequence. For example, when your child chooses a behavior that leads to losing her phone for 24 hours, have her place the phone on the kitchen counter and then carry on with your day as planned. No need for emotional withdrawal or acting sad or angry toward her. The relationship continues as before but the consequence stands. It's ok to express how you feel in appropriate ways. Try: "I feel_____ when _____. In the future I hope _____."

## Keep Some Consequences in Your Back Pocket

Do the baseboards need dusting or does your car need vacuuming? Keep that in mind and let it be a consequence for a concerning behavior. If a consequence makes your life more difficult you are less likely to provide the consistency with consequences that your child needs. So try to use consequences that will be beneficial to you rather than cumbersome.

Let natural consequences occur. If a choice has a natural, predictable and consistent consequence don't come up with your own. Let the natural consequence do the work for you. For example, not remembering to get important forms signed will result in your child not being able to participate in the activity that requires the signature of the parent. Don't work harder than your child to prevent natural consequences from occurring. These consequences are what will train the self-discipline and organization that you desperately want to see in your child.

# 6
# KEEP IT SIMPLE

Many parents can feel overwhelmed by the idea of shifting their thinking about how to parent. This approach is meant to simplify and not complicate the process of training children. In summary, the process of effectively training involves:

- Develop understanding about yourself as the parent and what you bring into parenting from your own family of origin. Some of these rules and beliefs will be helpful and effective and others will cause more conflict and complication. Knowing and understanding yourself will help sort out what needs to stay and what needs to change.
- Know your tendency to control instead of train. Having this clarity will help you make the choice in the moments that require your intervention with your child. Will you allow yourself to be drawn into controlling or will you choose to train despite the added effort it will require of you?
- Provide choices and consequences in the context of attending to your child's emotions. With this model, you are attending to your own emotions and the emotions of your child while providing structure that will train the child.

Questions to ask yourself to keep you oriented toward choices and consequences:
What's going on in me (thoughts and emotions) when I see my child behaving this way?

Should I act out of these thoughts and emotions of mine or should I process them within myself and then move on to train the behavior that is concerning me?

What behavior do I want to train?

What are my convictions related to that behavior?

What are the choices that my child has when it comes to that behavior?

What are the consequences of those behaviors?

Can I give those consequences consistently?

Can I provide the choices and their consequences without complicating the situation with my own emotional reactions?

Be honest with yourself. Acknowledge that training is slow and will not be easy or pretty but it has long term advantages that will serve your child for a lifetime. Keep it simple. Be consistent and let your child know how loved they are.

# 7
# FREQUENTLY ASKED QUESTIONS

**What are examples of consequences?**

These are divided into categories that may best fit the choices they address. For example, if a child has been disrespectful to a parent, the parent may choose a consequence from the relationship category.

Responsibility Consequences
- pulling weeds
- picking up limbs
- losing a device
- losing screen time
- wiping down surfaces (counters, light switches, doorknobs) in the home with a disinfecting wipe
- cleaning windows
- sweeping (inside or garage)
- vacuuming (house or car)
- missing time at the pool (or other exciting location)
- cook dinner for family

Relationship Consequences
- watching a movie with a parent instead of going out with friends

- parent coming to have lunch with a (middle school or high school) child
- making the beds for others in the family
- going to the grocery store as an assistant
- sitting in a quiet place like a porch that is away from people and distractions
- missing out on time with friends
- serving others (doing someone else's chore)
- volunteer with an organization/person who needs help
- going for a walk with a parent
- sitting with a parent on the porch, living room, etc. for a set amount of time
- spending a set amount of time in family area (not withdrawing to room, basement, etc.)
- play a boardgame with parents/family

When using any of these consequences, remember that the goal is to keep it simple and concise and to give the consequence with as little parental emotional reaction as possible.

Example: "Johnny, you chose to speak disrespectfully to your sister and you know that in our family when you choose to speak disrespectfully, you also choose to serve her by making her bed the next day."

Also remember that if the consequence is something that the parent actually desires (ex. having the car vacuumed) the parent is more likely to be consistent and follow through. If the consequence is cumbersome and difficult for the parent to implement or enforce the parent is more likely to be inconsistent, teaching the child that the parent will not follow-through. The child then learns his/her choices will not bring consequences.

**What if my child won't do the consequence?**

You simply, calmly and without a dramatic and emotional reaction, return to the five-step process of choices and consequences.

Parent: "Johnny, you choose to speak disrespectfully to your sister and you know that in our family when you choose to speak disrespectfully, you also choose to serve her by making her bed the next day."

Johnny: "Yeah right. I didn't choose that and I'm not going to make her bed tomorrow."

Parent: "Johnny, you can choose to not make your sister's bed tomorrow. You know that when you choose to argue with a parent in our family you are choosing to miss going to a friend's house this weekend. I'll let you decide what you want to do about making the bed tomorrow."

Keep in mind that the child may do the consequence with a bad attitude. Attitude is the condition of his/her heart being expressed through face and body language (and sometimes language). We can't train the heart. We can only train behavior and pray that the One who created the child's heart will change it. When the heart changes, so will the attitude. If you engage in demanding that a child accept a consequence with a smile and a skip, you are signing up for a power struggle that won't end well.

**What if my kid is running into the street while playing? I should let her risk her life just to train her with choices and consequences?**

Of course not. There are times to control and this would be one of those times. But know that when you choose to control you are preventing or changing a behavior now but it will not have the long term impact of training. You would grab your child and prevent them from running into the street (control) and then return to your five steps of training. See it broken down here:

1. Identify your Conviction: Making Safe Choices Near Traffic

2. Keep it to yourself-self talk: "Even though I am scared and worried after watching my child run toward the street, I will not spend five minutes lecturing on all that could have happened and all the related information I have about children and traffic. My child

will not listen and I will become frustrated. Instead, I will teach my child about safety through choices and consequences."

3. Show grace: "You really scared me when you ran to the road. I will draw a line in the driveway and that will be your reminder not to get so close to the street. If you choose to go past the line you will be choosing to play in the house today and tomorrow and not play in the driveway."

4. Allow the Choice. Don't remind, nag and beg. Keep a watchful eye and if/when she steps over that line let her know she has chosen to play inside today and tomorrow.

5. Provide the Consequence. Pack up the scooters and helmets, basketballs and sidewalk chalk and head in for two days of indoor play. When she asks if she can play outside calmly and patiently remind her that she chose to play inside when she stepped over the line in the driveway.

## How do I stay "emotionally connected" while providing choices and consequences?

Managing your own emotional reactions to a child's behavior is the first step of staying connected. Acting out anger creates distance, so when we deal with each other without angry reactions it is easier to stay connected. Helping the child identify his/her emotions related to what is going on is helpful too. The child will feel understood because the parent gives attention to feeling and not just behavior. This could sound like "Susie, I see you are slamming doors and stomping your feet. I think that choosing to help with chores for 20 minutes (the consequence she chooses with her behavior) is disappointing and frustrating to you. I know that it hurts to feel disappointment and frustration."

## Can my typically compliant child also benefit from training with this model?

Even compliant children will present parents with opportunities to train when their behavior becomes concerning or confusing. While compliant children make it easier to live life (ie. they do what you want them to do when you want them to do it), this doesn't mean they will leave home trained in good decision making. Looking for opportunities to train compliant children in understanding the choice-consequence connection is just as important as training the strong-willed or defiant child.

# 8
# QUICK REFERENCE GUIDE

**Parental Insight**

1. Experiences in your family of origin impact who you are, how you parent and how you function in relationships.
2. How you interpret (think and understand) the world is based on your family experience.
3. Knowing these things helps you make informed and healthy choices in parenting.

**Application**

1. Identify your convictions in parenting/relationships and keep them to yourself (don't lecture and argue).
2. Identify the behavior that needs to be trained (become clear about what you are focused on and NOT focused on). Become intentional about how you will address this concerning behavior.
3. Communicate with grace about behavior that is being trained and help others know the consequences for this behavior in the future. Don't give consequences until others have been informed about the choices they have. This decreases resentment and conflict and increases understanding and mutual respect.

4. Allow the choice (don't control, nag, lecture, etc.).
5. Give the consequence consistently. Let the consequence be the consequence, not your emotional reactivity.
6. Stay faithful to the process.

Knowing your choices and the resulting consequences gives you the structure and power to grow.

When parenting out of insight and not control, children and their parents have the opportunity to behave better because everyone is growing in insight and applicable skills.

# NOTES

## Chapter 2

1.  Kevin Leman, *The Birth Order Book* (Grand Rapids: Revell, 1998), 15.

2.  Taken from *Love Is A Choice* by Robert Hemfelt, Frank Minirth and Paul Meier Copyright © 1989 by Robert Hemfelt, Frank Minirth and Paul Meier. Used by permission of Thomas Nelson. www.thomasnelson.com.

3.  By permission. From Merriam-Webster.com ©2019 by Merriam-Webster, Inc. https://www.merriam-webster.com/dictionary/scapegoat.

Made in the USA
Monee, IL
15 February 2020

21752732R00030